Mr McGee
AND THE
Blackberry Jam
Pamela Allen

To Judith
and our memory of
the Drury cow

Puffin Books

Published by the Penguin Group
Penguin Books Australia Ltd
250 Camberwell Road
Camberwell, Victoria 3124, Australia
Penguin Books Ltd
80 Strand, London WC2R 0RL, England
Penguin Putnam Inc.
375 Hudson Street, New York, New York 10014, USA
Penguin Books, a division of Pearson Canada
10 Alcorn Avenue, Toronto, Ontario, Canada, M4V 3B2
Penguin Books (N.Z.) Ltd
Cnr Rosedale and Airborne Roads, Albany, Auckland, New Zealand
Penguin Books (South Africa) (Pty) Ltd
24 Sturdee Avenue, Rosebank, Johannesburg 2196, South Africa
Penguin Books India (P) Ltd
11, Community Centre, Panchsheel Park, New Delhi 110 017, India

First published by Penguin Books Australia, 1993
Published in Picture Puffin 1994

15 17 19 21 23 25 24 22 20 18 16 14

© Pamela Allen, 1993

The moral right of the author has been asserted

Designed by Deborah Brash/Brash Design
Typeset in 26pt Century Oldstyle by Post Typesetters
Made and printed in China by Everbest
National Library of Australia
Cataloguing-in-Publication data:

Allen, Pamela
Mr McGee and the Blackberry jam.
ISBN 0 14 054501 8.

1. Children's poetry, Australian. I. Title.
A821.3

www.puffin.com.au

Mr McGee
AND THE
Blackberry Jam
Pamela Allen

Puffin Books

Underneath this apple tree
lives a man called Mr McGee.

This morning he was feeling grumpy.
He'd made the porridge and it was lumpy.

He'd put two sugars in his tea,
then spilt the lot and burnt his knee.

When he went to butter his bread,
he found the butter too hard to spread.
So it wasn't surprising when he said,

'I HATE MARMALADE,
I WANT BLACKBERRY JAM INSTEAD!'

So off he went with his billy can

to find the blackberries for his jam.

He walked and walked for quite a while
until he came upon a stile.

Guess what he could see from there?

Blackberries, blackberries everywhere.

Shouting, 'Look what I have found,'
he took one leap on to the ground

so he could pick those big round berries,
black and fat and big as cherries.

One by one in the billy they dropped.

He liked the sound of PLIP, PLOP, PLOPPED.

Now . . . while he picked so busily,
behind him where he couldn't see,

a herd of heifers gathered round
to view the stranger they had found.

When Mr McGee discovered them there,
he blurted out,

'I've washed my hands, I've combed my hair,
oh, come on girls, you're not being fair,
you know that it is rude to stare.'

He turned his back and went on picking,
and that was when they started licking.

All their tongues went in and out
up and down and round about.

Mr McGee began to squirm
as though he were a little worm.

'Stop it! Please! You're tickling me.'
And then he giggled helplessly.

'Ha, Ha, Ha! Ho, Ho, Ho! He, He, He!
Ha, Ha, Ha! Ho, Ho, Ho! He, He, He!'

Just like a kookaburra's song,
the laughing noise went on and on.

The bull let out a mighty bellow,
'Get out of here, you cheeky fellow!'

The startled heifers all turned round.
The bull was pawing at the ground.

Mr McGee just turned to stone.
He couldn't run or move a bone.

One moment he was standing there,

the next ... he was tossed into the air.

As he soared above the crowd
he just had time to shout out loud,

'I think the lot of you are rotten!'
Then both his hands clutched at his bottom.

He landed softly in a heap
on the back of a woolly sheep.

He rode the sheep just like a horse
and got home really fast, of course.

That night, when he was safe in bed,
he thought about his day, then said,
'I can't think *what* got in my head.

IT'S MARMALADE I LOVE ON BREAD!'